KIM SCHAEFER

Quilts
from textured solids

20 RICH PROJECTS TO PIECE & APPLIQUÉ

C&T PUBLISHING

Text copyright © 2011 by Kim Schaefer

Artwork copyright © 2011 by C&T Publishing, Inc.

Publisher: Amy Marson

Copyeditor/Proofreader: Wordfirm Inc.

Creative Director: Gailen Runge

Cover/Book Designer: Kerry Graham

Acquisitions Editor: Susanne Woods

Production Coordinator: Jenny Leicester

Editor: Lynn Koolish

Production Editor: Julia Cianci

Technical Editors: Helen Frost and Sandy Peterson

Illustrator: Richard Sheppard

Photography by Christina Carty-Francis and Diane Pedersen of C&T Publishing, Inc., unless otherwise noted

Published by C&T Publishing, Inc., P.O. Box 1456, Lafayette, CA 94549

Library of Congress Cataloging-in-Publication Data

Schaefer, Kim, 1960-

   Quilts from textured solids : 20 rich projects to piece & appliqué / Kim Schaefer.

      p. cm.

   ISBN 978-1-60705-198-5 (softcover)

   1. Patchwork--Patterns. 2. Appliqué--Patterns. 3. Textured woven fabrics. 4. Quilts. I. Title.

   TT835.S2844 2011

   746.46--dc22

                              2010033970

Printed in China

10 9 8 7 6 5 4 3 2 1

Acknowledgments

I am so fortunate to work with C&T Publishing. I am honored to work with such a creative and talented team. Special thanks to my editor, Lynn Koolish, who makes the whole process a pleasure.

A very special thank-you to my technical editor, Helen Frost. Helen has the difficult job of checking my patterns for accuracy. I am grateful to have someone so competent and thorough. Thank you for finding and fixing my many mistakes.

Thank you to the very talented Richard Sheppard for the beautiful illustrations.

A huge thank-you to my longarm quilter extraordinaire, Diane Minkley of Patched Works, Inc. Thank you for finishing my quilts beautifully and with such artistic flair. You are a talented and creative quilter, and your quilting absolutely shines in this book.

All the fabrics used in this book are from my very own Tic Tac line with Andover/Makower Fabrics. Special thanks to everyone at Andover for their support and encouragement and for providing such great fabrics to work with.

Thank you also to my great husband, Gary Schaefer, for transcribing to disc yet again another book for me.

Last but not least, special thanks to my button brigade. My mom, Alice Sanders; dad, Jerry Sanders; sisters, Jill Sanders Trachte and Kelly Sanders; and niece, Sara Sanders, have all contributed to my button collection over the years.

Contents

Introduction

I have always been attracted to quilts made from solid fabrics, and I am especially inspired by these quilts. There is a boldness and beauty in the quilts that is timeless. The lack of pattern in the fabrics allows the viewer to focus on the design of the quilt and the actual quilting.

Almost every quilt shop has a great selection of solids or textured solids to choose from. They are basics for a reason. Quilts made from these fabrics have withstood the test of time. Often quilts made from solid fabrics have a contemporary feeling regardless of when they were made. They are not dated the way quilts made from printed fabrics can be. Solid fabrics can be exciting and make for some stunning quilts. Many of the projects will enable you to experiment with color and explore the endless possibilities that can be created using solid fabrics.

This book contains a variety of projects: lap quilts, wall quilts, tabletop quilts, and mini-quilts in both pieced and appliquéd designs for you to choose from.

I love buttons and have collected them for years. The solid fabrics in these quilts seemed to be perfect for showing off some of my favorite buttons. I have embellished several of the projects with a variety of these buttons.

I have enjoyed designing and making this collection of projects, and I hope that they will be a source of creativity and inspiration to you as well.

General Instructions

Rotary Cutting

I recommend that you cut all the fabrics used in the pieced blocks, borders, and bindings with a rotary cutter, an acrylic ruler, and a cutting mat. Trim the blocks and borders with these tools as well.

Piecing

All piecing measurements include ¼" seam allowances. If you sew an accurate ¼" seam, you will succeed! My biggest and best quiltmaking tip is to learn to sew an accurate ¼" seam.

Pressing

Press seams to one side, preferably toward the darker fabric. Press flat, and avoid sliding the iron over the pieces, which can distort and stretch them. When you join two seamed sections, press the seams in opposite directions so you can nest the seams and reduce bulk.

Appliqué

All the appliqué instructions are for paper-backed fusible web with machine appliqué, and all the appliqué patterns have been drawn in reverse. If you prefer a different appliqué method, you will need to trace a mirror image of the pattern and add seam allowances to the appliqué pieces. A lightweight paper-backed fusible web works best for machine appliqué. Choose your favorite fusible web, and follow the manufacturer's directions.

general appliqué instructions

1. Trace all the parts of the appliqué design on the paper side of the fusible web. Trace each layer of the design separately. For example, trace all the petals on a flower as one piece, and trace the center as another. Whenever two shapes in the design butt together, overlap them by about ⅛" to help prevent the potential of a gap between them. When tracing the shapes, extend the underlapped edge ⅛" beyond the drawn edge in the pattern. Write the pattern letter or number on each traced shape.

2. Cut around the appliqué shapes, leaving a ¼" margin around each one.

3. Iron each fusible web shape to the wrong side of the appropriate fabric, following the manufacturer's instructions for fusing. I don't worry about the grainline when placing the pieces. Cut on the traced lines, and peel off the paper backing. A thin layer of fusible web will remain on the wrong side of the fabric. This layer will adhere the appliqué pieces to the backgrounds.

4. Position the pieces on the backgrounds. Press to fuse them in place.

5. Machine stitch around the appliqué pieces using a zigzag, satin, or blanket stitch. Stitch any detail lines indicated on the patterns.

My choice is the satin stitch. I generally use beige thread for all the stitching. Sometimes the stitches blend with the fabric, and sometimes they don't. Using one color throughout gives the quilt a folk art look. However, on *Tequila Sunrise* (page 12) and *Connect the Dots* (page 23), I used matching threads. You can see how changing the thread color changes the entire look of the quilt. As always, the type of stitching you use and the thread color you select are personal choices.

Putting It All Together

When all the blocks are completed for a project, lay them out on the floor or, if you are lucky enough to have one, a design wall. Arrange and rearrange the blocks until you are happy with the overall look. Each project has specific directions as well as diagrams and photos for assembly.

Borders

If the quilt borders or lattice pieces need to be longer than 40", join crosswise strips of fabric at a 45° angle as necessary, and cut the strips to the desired length. All borders in the book are straight cut; none of them have mitered corners.

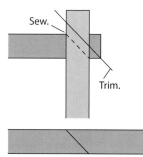

Sew. Trim. Join borders with 45° angle.

Layering the Quilt

Cut the batting and backing pieces 4"–5" larger than the quilt top. Place the pressed backing on the bottom, right side down. Place the batting over the backing and the quilt top on top, right side up. Make sure all the layers are flat and smooth and the quilt top is centered over the batting and backing. Pin or baste the quilt.

Note: If you are going to have your top quilted by a longarm quilter, contact her for specific batting and backing requirements, which may differ from the instructions above.

Since I prefer not to piece the backing for the table runners, the fabric amounts allow for the length of the runner. I add the leftover fabric to my stash.

Quilting

Quilting is a personal choice; you may prefer hand or machine quilting. My favorite method is to send the quilt top to a longarm quilter. This method keeps my number of unfinished tops low and the number of finished quilts high.

Buttons

Adding buttons to the quilts is optional. I add them after the quilting is finished. Sewing the buttons on by machine is quick and professional looking.

Color and Fabric Choices

I have used 100% cotton fabrics in all the projects in this book. I find they are easy to work with and readily available at local quilt shops.

For this book I chose to use all textured solids, also known as tone-on-tone fabrics. Although the textured solids have some variation in color, visually they read as solids. It was both interesting and rewarding for me as a designer to work with these fabrics. I did not feel that limiting myself to the textured solids in any way limited design possibilities.

I have a very relaxed approach to color and fabric choices, and although I have been trained in color theory, I feel that most of my choices are intuitive. I use a design wall and usually "play" with the fabrics before I sew them. If you are new to quilting or feel unsure of your color choices, one thing I have found is that generally the more fabrics I use in a quilt, the more I like it.

Thankfully, everyone has different tastes and preferences when it comes to color. In the end it is your quilt and your choice, and what's important is that it's visually pleasing to you.

Make the Quilt Your Own

If you want to change the size of a quilt, simply add or subtract blocks, or change the width of the borders. Many times eliminating a border will give the quilt a more modern, contemporary look. Your color choices may be totally different from mine.

Yardage and Fabric Requirements

I have given yardage and fabric requirements for each project, many calling for a total amount of assorted fabrics that can be used as a base for your quilt. The yardage amounts may vary depending on several factors: the size of the quilt, the number of fabrics used, and the number of pieces you cut from each fabric. Always cut the pieces for the patchwork first, then cut any appliqué pieces.

The amounts given for binding fabric allow for 2"-wide strips cut on the straight of grain. I usually use the same fabric for backing and binding, as it's a good way to use leftover fabric. Cut the binding strips either on the crosswise or lengthwise grain of the leftover fabric, whichever will yield the longest strips.

Gator's
Lap Quilt

{ *My son Gator claimed this quilt while it was still on my design wall, thus the title Gator's Quilt. The swirling quilting motif enhances the simple design of the quilt.* }

Quilted by Diane Minkley of Patched Works, Inc.

MATERIALS

6¼ yards total assorted greens, blues, and teals for pieced blocks and outer pieced border

⅔ yard black for inner border and outer pieced border

4¾ yards for backing and binding

⅝ yard for binding if different from backing

67″ × 83″ batting

CUTTING

Cut from assorted greens, blues, and teals:

- 63 rectangles 1½″ × 8½″ for pieced blocks
- 63 rectangles 1¾″ × 8½″ for pieced blocks
- 63 rectangles 2″ × 8½″ for pieced blocks
- 63 rectangles 2¼″ × 8½″ for pieced blocks
- 63 rectangles 3″ × 8½″ for pieced blocks
- 34 rectangles 2½″ × 6½″ for outer pieced border

Cut from black:

- 2 strips 1½″ × 72½″ for 2 side inner borders *
- 2 strips 1½″ × 58½″ for top and bottom inner borders *
- 34 squares 2½″ × 2½″ for outer pieced border

* Cut 7 strips 1½″ × fabric width, piece the strips end to end (see Borders, page 6), and cut the border pieces.

Piecing

Sew 1 each of the following rectangles together, in random order, to make a pieced block:

1½″ × 8½″

1¾″ × 8½″

2″ × 8½″

2¼″ × 8½″

3″ × 8½″

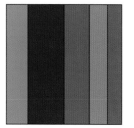

Make 63.
Finished size: 8″ × 8″

Note: Each block will be different because the rectangles are sewn in random order, but the blocks will measure 8½″ × 8½″ including the seam allowance.

Putting It All Together

Refer to Putting It All Together diagram (at right).

quilt center

Arrange and sew together the blocks in 9 rows of 7 blocks each. Sew together the rows. Press.

inner border

1. Sew the 2 side borders to the quilt top. Press toward the borders.

2. Sew the top and bottom borders to the quilt top. Press toward the borders.

outer pieced border

1. Arrange and sew together 10 squares 2½″ × 2½″ and 9 rectangles 2½″ × 6½″ for the 2 side borders.

2. Sew the 2 side borders to the quilt top. Press.

3. Arrange and sew together 8 rectangles 2½″ × 6½″ and 7 squares 2½″ × 2½″ for the top and bottom borders. Press.

4. Sew the top and bottom borders to the quilt top. Press.

finishing

1. Layer the quilt with batting and backing. Baste or pin. See Layering the Quilt (page 6).

2. Quilt as desired, and bind.

Putting It All Together

Vine Climb
— Lap Quilt —

Soft backgrounds set the stage for climbing appliquéd flowers and vines in this traditional quilt with a romantic flavor. Use one green fabric for the leaves, or piece several greens together for more interest.

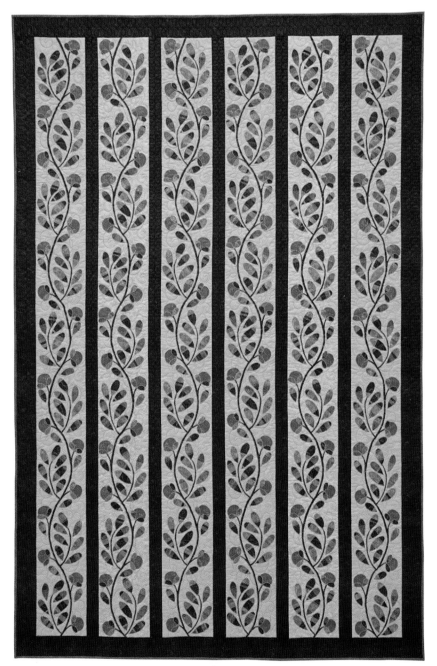

Quilted by Diane Minkley of Patched Works, Inc.

🌸 MATERIALS

2⅝ yards light for appliqué backgrounds

2⅝ yards light cream for appliqué backgrounds

2⅝ yards burgundy for lattice and border

2⅝ yards dark green for vines

2½ yards total assorted greens for pieced leaves or 1¼ yards of 1 green

¾ yard pink for flowers

8 yards paper-backed fusible web

5¾ yards for backing and binding

⅝ yard for binding if different from backing

69″ × 101″ batting

🌸 CUTTING

Cut pieces on lengthwise grain of fabric.

Cut from light: 4 strips 8½″ × 90½″ for appliqué backgrounds

Cut from light cream: 2 strips 8½″ × 90½″ for appliqué backgrounds

Cut from burgundy:

- 5 strips 2½″ × 90½″ for lattice
- 2 strips 3½″ × 90½″ for 2 side borders
- 2 strips 3½″ × 64½″ for top and bottom borders

To prepare the fabric for the pieced leaf appliqués, cut the assorted greens in strips that vary in width from ¾″ to 2½″ × the width of the fabric. Sew the strips together in random order, and press. The number of strips you will need varies depending on the number of fabrics used and the amount you cut from each.

Appliqué

1. Cut 2 pieces of paper 8″ × 90″. Measure and mark lines every 10″. Trace the pattern on pattern pullout pages P73–P80, aligning the marked lines with the dotted lines between each repeat of the pattern. Trace pattern piece 1 to make a full pattern. For Row A, begin with the bottom repeat. For Row B, begin with the top repeat.

2. Use the traced patterns and the patterns on the pullout pages to cut:

3 and 3 reverse of pattern piece 1

27 and 27 reverse of pattern pieces 2 through 15

24 and 24 reverse of pattern piece 16

3. Appliqué the appropriate pieces onto the backgrounds.

Putting It All Together

Refer to Putting It All Together diagram (below).

quilt center

Sew the lattice strips between the appliqué backgrounds. Press.

border

1. Sew the 2 side borders to the quilt top. Press toward the borders.

2. Sew the top and bottom borders to the quilt top. Press toward the borders.

finishing

1. Layer the quilt with batting and backing. Baste or pin. See Layering the Quilt (page 6).

2. Quilt as desired, and bind.

Putting It All Together

Row A; make 3.   Row B; make 3.

Tequila Sunrise

——— Lap Quilt ———

{ *This quilt glows with a spectacular show of color. Super simple appliqué shapes make this quilt a great choice for first-time appliqué.* }

Quilted by Diane Minkley of Patched Works, Inc.

MATERIALS

5 yards total assorted brights for appliqué backgrounds and pieced outer border

3½ yards total assorted brights for appliqué pieces

¾ yard black for inner border

7½ yards paper-backed fusible web

5¼ yards for backing and binding

⅝ yard for binding if different from backing

71″ × 91″ batting

CUTTING

Cut from assorted brights: 192 squares 5½″ × 5½″ for appliqué backgrounds

Cut from assorted brights: 100 rectangles 1½″ × 3½″ for pieced outer border

Cut from black:

- 2 strips 2½″ × 80½″ for 2 side inner borders *
- 2 strips 2½″ × 64½″ for top and bottom inner borders *

* Cut 8 strips 2½″ × fabric width, piece the strips end to end (see Borders, page 6), and cut the border pieces.

Appliqué

1. Use the patterns on pattern pullout page P73–P80 to cut 192 each of pattern pieces 1 through 4. *Note:* The pattern pieces include the seam allowance for the outer edges of the block. Pieces 1–3 extend under Piece 4.

2. Appliqué the appropriate pieces to the backgrounds. Make 192 blocks.

Appliqué blocks. Make 192.

Putting It All Together

Refer to Putting It All Together diagram (at right).

quilt center

1. Arrange and sew together the blocks in 16 rows of 12 blocks each. Press.

2. Sew together the rows to form the quilt center. Press.

inner border

1. Sew the 2 side borders to the quilt top. Press toward the borders.

2. Sew the top and bottom borders to the quilt top. Press toward the borders.

outer pieced border

1. Arrange and sew together 2 rows of 28 rectangles 1½″ × 3½″ for the 2 side borders. Press.

2. Sew the 2 side borders to the quilt top. Press toward the borders.

3. Arrange and sew together 2 rows of 22 rectangles 1½″ × 3½″ for the top and bottom borders. Press.

4. Sew the top and bottom borders to the quilt top. Press toward the borders.

finishing

1. Layer the quilt with batting and backing. Baste or pin. See Layering the Quilt (page 6).

2. Quilt as desired, and bind.

Putting It All Together

First Steps
Lap Quilt

*Simple squares and rectangles make up the center of this quilt.
The soft color palette makes this an easy quilt to live with.*

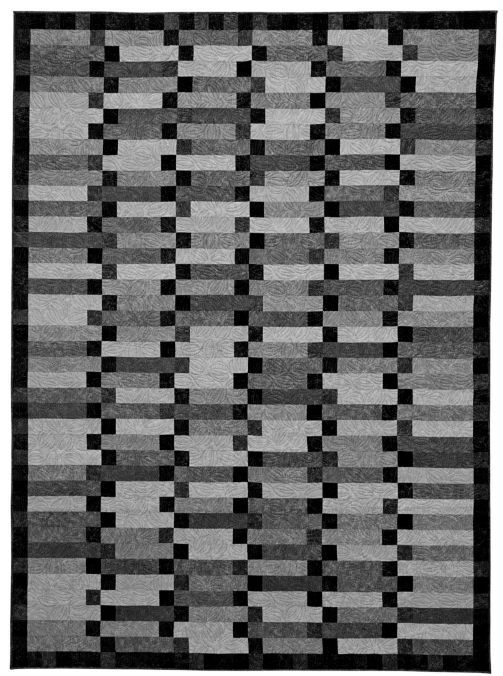

Quilted by Diane Minkley of Patched Works, Inc.

◼ MATERIALS

4½ yards total assorted lights for quilt center

1¾ yards total assorted darks for quilt center and border

5⅛ yards for backing and binding

⅝ yard for binding if different from backing

69" × 89" batting

◼ CUTTING

Cut from assorted lights for quilt center:

- 40 rectangles 2½" × 10½"
- 200 rectangles 2½" × 8½"

Cut from assorted darks: 344 squares 2½" × 2½"
for quilt center and border

Piecing

Referring to the Putting It All Together
diagram (at right), arrange and sew
together the rectangles and squares
into 6 vertical rows for the quilt
center. Press.

Putting It All Together

*Refer to Putting It All Together diagram
(at right).*

quilt center

Arrange and sew together the
rows. Press.

pieced border

1. Arrange and sew together 2 rows
of 40 squares each for the 2 side borders. Press.

2. Sew the side borders to the quilt
top. Press toward the borders.

3. Arrange and sew together 2 rows
of 32 squares each for the top and
bottom borders. Press.

4. Sew the top and bottom borders
to the quilt top. Press toward the
borders.

finishing

1. Layer the quilt with batting and backing. Baste or pin.
See Layering the Quilt (page 6).

2. Quilt as desired, and bind.

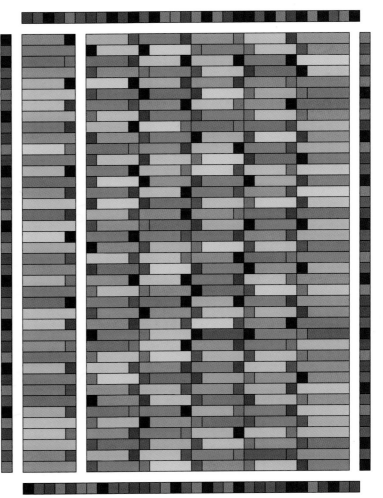

Putting It All Together

Funky Flowers
Lap Quilt

{ *Rich, earthy background colors provide the base for this quilt and allow the funky teal flowers to create the visual impact. A simple pieced border frames the quilt body.* }

Quilted by Diane Minkley of Patched Works, Inc.

◆ MATERIALS

4 yards total assorted grays, browns, and lights for appliqué backgrounds, pieced rows, and borders

2⅛ yards black for lattice strips, inner border, and flower pistils

2 yards total assorted teals and greens for flowers, leaves, stems, and pieced outer border

2¼ yards paper-backed fusible web

4⅞ yards for backing and binding

⅝ yard for binding if different from backing

69″ × 85″ batting

◆ CUTTING

Cut pieces on lengthwise grain of fabric.

Cut from assorted grays, browns, and lights for backgrounds and pieced rows:

- 22 rectangles 4½″ × 5½″
- 11 rectangles 4½″ × 6½″
- 11 rectangles 4½″ × 7½″
- 11 rectangles 4½″ × 8½″
- 22 rectangles 4½″ × 9½″
- 11 rectangles 4½″ × 10½″
- 11 rectangles 4½″ × 11½″

Cut from black:

- 12 strips 1½″ × 70½″ for lattice and 2 side inner borders
- 2 strips 1½″ × 56½″ for top and bottom inner borders

Cut from the assorted grays, browns, greens, and teals: 136 rectangles 2½″ × 4½″ for pieced outer border

Appliqué

1. Use the patterns on pattern pullout pages P73–P80 to cut:

    7 each of pattern pieces 1 through 6

    11 each of pattern pieces 7 through 12

2. Appliqué the appropriate pieces onto the backgrounds.

9″ block; make 11.

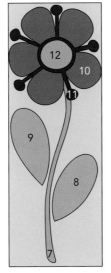

11″ block; make 7.

Putting It All Together

Refer to Putting It All Together diagram (page 18).

quilt center

1. Arrange and sew together the appliqué blocks and pieces into 11 vertical rows. Press.

2. Sew the lattice strips between the vertical rows. Press.

inner border

1. Sew the 2 side borders to the quilt top. Press toward the borders.

2. Sew the top and bottom borders to the quilt top. Press toward the borders.

outer pieced border

1. Arrange and sew together 2 rows of 36 rectangles 2½″ × 4½″ for the 2 side borders. Press.

2. Sew the 2 side borders to the quilt top. Press toward the borders.

3. Arrange and sew together 2 rows of 32 rectangles 2½″ × 4½″ for the top and bottom borders. Press.

4. Sew the top and bottom borders to the quilt top. Press toward the borders.

finishing

1. Layer the quilt with batting and backing. Baste or pin. See Layering the Quilt (page 6).

2. Quilt as desired, and bind.

Putting It All Together

QUILTS FROM TEXTURED SOLIDS

Seven Happy Flowers

— Wall Quilt —

These happy flowers will just make you smile! Embellish with your favorite buttons for added visual interest.

Quilted by Diane Minkley of Patched Works, Inc.

MATERIALS

½ yard light for appliqué background

⅛ yard light green for inner border

⅓ yard dark green for outer border

¾ yard total assorted brights for flowers

½ yard total assorted greens for stems and leaves

¼ yard black for flowers

2 yards paper-backed fusible web

1⅜ yards for backing and binding

⅜ yard for binding if different from backing

48″ × 23″ batting

50 (approximately) buttons (optional)

CUTTING

Cut from light: 1 rectangle 39½″ × 14½″ for appliqué background

Cut from light green:

- 2 strips 1″ × 14½″ for 2 side inner borders
- 2 strips 1″ × 40½″ for top and bottom inner borders

Cut from dark green:

- 2 strips 2″ × 15½″ for 2 side outer borders
- 2 strips 2″ × 43½″ for top and bottom outer borders *

* Cut 3 strips 2″ × fabric width, piece the strips end to end (see Borders, page 6), and cut the border pieces.

Putting It All Together

Refer to Putting It All Together diagram (at right).

inner border

1. Sew the 2 side borders to the background. Press toward the borders.

2. Sew the top and bottom borders to the background. Press toward the borders.

outer border

1. Sew the 2 side borders to the quilt top. Press toward the borders.

2. Sew the top and bottom borders to the quilt top. Press toward the borders.

appliqué

1. Use the patterns on pattern pullout pages P65–P72 and P73–P80 to cut:

    1 each of pattern pieces 1 through 73

    7 each of pattern pieces 74 and 75

2. Mark along the bottom inner border to place the appliqué pieces. Measure and mark 4½″ from the sides of the background, and then measure and mark every 5″. Place a flower stem on each mark to position the flowers.

3. Appliqué the appropriate pieces onto the quilt top.

finishing

1. Layer the quilt with batting and backing. Baste or pin. See Layering the Quilt (page 6).

2. Quilt as desired, and bind.

3. Add buttons if desired.

Putting It All Together

Simple Stripes
Wall Quilt

Simple stripes make up the body of this bold wall quilt. Cut the strips on the lengthwise grain to make straight strips without seams and with lots of leftovers! The beautiful longarm quilting enhances the simplicity of the design.

Quilted by Diane Minkley of Patched Works, Inc.

MATERIALS

1½ yards each light gray, dark gray, burgundy, teal, dark green, light green, red, and peach for pieced center and outer border corner squares

1½ yards dark teal for inner border

⅛ yard light teal for inner border corner squares

1⅝ yards brown for outer border

4⅛ yards for backing and binding

⅝ yard for binding if different from backing

71″ × 71″ batting

CUTTING

Cut pieces on lengthwise grain of fabric.

Cut from light gray: 1 strip 2½″ × 50½″ for pieced center

Cut from dark gray: 2 strips 4½″ × 50½″ for pieced center

Cut from burgundy: 4 strips 2½″ × 50½″ for pieced center

Cut from teal: 2 strips 2½″ × 50½″ for pieced center

Cut from dark green: 2 strips 4½″ × 50½″ for pieced center

Cut from light green: 4 strips 2½″ × 50½″ for pieced center

Cut from red: 2 strips 3½″ × 50½″ for pieced center

Cut from peach: 2 strips 3½″ × 50½″ for pieced center and 4 squares 6½″ × 6½″ for outer border corners

Cut from light teal: 4 squares 2½″ × 2½″ for inner border corners

Cut from dark teal: 4 strips 2½″ × 50½″ for inner borders

Cut from brown: 4 strips 6½″ × 54½″ for outer border

Putting It All Together

Refer to Putting It All Together diagram (at right).

quilt center

Arrange and sew together the strips to form the quilt center. Press.

inner border

1. Sew the 2 side borders to the quilt top. Press toward the borders.

2. Sew a 2½″ × 2½″ square on each end of the remaining inner borders. Press.

3. Sew the top and bottom inner borders to the quilt top. Press toward the borders.

outer border

1. Sew the 2 side borders to the quilt top. Press toward the borders.

2. Sew a 6½″ × 6½″ square on each end of the remaining outer borders. Press.

3. Sew the top and bottom outer borders to the quilt top. Press toward the borders.

finishing

1. Layer the quilt with batting and backing. Baste or pin. See Layering the Quilt (page 6).

2. Quilt as desired, and bind.

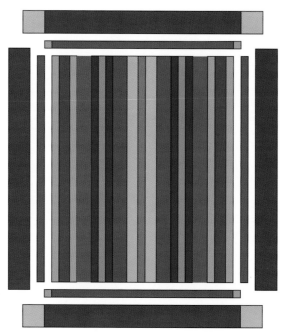

Putting It All Together

Finished block size: 6" × 6"

Finished wall quilt: 54½" × 54½"

Connect the Dots
── Wall Quilt ──

Vibrant colors and a simple border of appliquéd circles give an updated, fresh look to the traditional favorite Rail Fence block.

Quilted by Diane Minkley of Patched Works, Inc.

MATERIALS

¼ yard light purple for pieced blocks and appliquéd circles

⅛ yard dark purple for pieced blocks

⅓ yard light red for pieced blocks and appliquéd circles

⅓ yard dark red for pieced blocks and appliqué backgrounds

½ yard light orange for pieced blocks and appliquéd circles

½ yard dark orange for pieced blocks and appliqué backgrounds

⅝ yard light yellow for pieced blocks and appliquéd circles

⅝ yard dark yellow for pieced blocks and appliqué backgrounds

⅝ yard light green for pieced blocks and appliquéd circles

⅝ yard dark green for pieced blocks and appliqué backgrounds

¼ yard light teal for pieced blocks

⅓ yard dark teal for pieced blocks and appliqué backgrounds

¼ yard light blue for pieced blocks

⅛ yard dark blue for pieced blocks

1⅜ yards paper-backed fusible web

3½ yards for backing and binding

½ yard for binding if different from backing

59″ × 59″ batting

CUTTING

Cut the following rectangles 2½″x 6½″ for pieced blocks:

- 2 from light purple
- 1 from dark purple
- 8 from light red
- 16 from light orange
- 24 from light yellow
- 24 from light green
- 16 from light teal
- 8 from light blue
- 4 from dark blue

Cut from dark red:

- 4 rectangles 2½″ × 6½″ for pieced blocks
- 4 squares 6½″ × 6½″ for appliqué backgrounds

Cut from dark orange:

- 8 rectangles 2½″ × 6½″ for pieced blocks
- 8 squares 6½″ × 6½″ for appliqué backgrounds

Cut from dark yellow:

- 12 rectangles 2½″ × 6½″ for pieced blocks
- 8 squares 6½″ × 6½″ for appliqué backgrounds

Cut from dark green:

- 12 rectangles 2½″ × 6½″ for pieced blocks
- 8 squares 6½″ × 6½″ for appliqué backgrounds

Cut from dark teal:

- 8 rectangles 2½″ × 6½″ for pieced blocks
- 4 squares 6½″ × 6½″ for appliqué backgrounds

Appliqué

1. Use the patterns on pattern pullout pages P61–P64 to cut 32 of pattern piece 1.

2. Cut 4 each of light purple and light green and 8 each of light red, light orange, and light yellow.

3. Appliqué the circles onto the backgrounds.

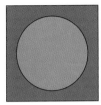

Make 32.

Piecing

Make the following blocks: 1 purple, 4 red, 4 blue, 8 teal, 8 orange, 12 green, and 12 yellow. Then, press.

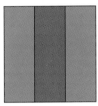

Piece blocks. Make 49.

Putting It All Together

Refer to Putting It All Together diagram (at right).

quilt center

1. Sew together the blocks in 7 rows of 7 blocks each. Press.

2. Sew together the rows. Press.

appliquéd border

1. Arrange and sew together 2 rows of 7 appliqué blocks for the 2 side borders. Press.

2. Sew the 2 side borders to the quilt top. Press toward the borders.

3. Arrange and sew together 2 rows of 9 appliqué blocks for the top and bottom borders. Press.

4. Sew the top and bottom borders to the quilt top. Press toward the borders.

finishing

1. Layer the quilt with batting and backing. Baste or pin. See Layering the Quilt (page 6).

2. Quilt as desired, and bind.

Putting It All Together

Totally Square
Wall Quilt

Totally Square is a fun and easy quilt to make. With a contemporary feel, it's perfect for today's modern quilter. The center square of each block is surrounded by one, two, or three rings of color, each made from a set of four rectangles.

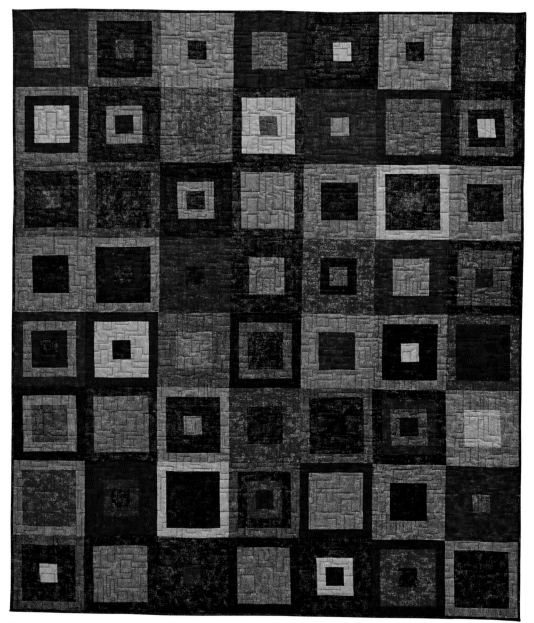

Quilted by Diane Minkley of Patched Works, Inc.

MATERIALS

5 yards total assorted teals, reds, grays, browns, and tans for pieced blocks

3⅝ yards for backing and binding

½ yard for binding if different from backing

61" × 69" batting

CUTTING

The pieces for each matching set of squares and rectangles are listed together.

Cut for block A:

- 11 squares 6½" × 6½" for centers

- 22 rectangles 1½" × 6½" and 22 rectangles 1½" × 8½"

Cut for block B:

- 12 squares 2½" × 2½" for centers

- 24 squares 2½" × 2½" and 24 rectangles 2½" × 6½"

- 24 rectangles 1½" × 6½" and 24 rectangles 1½" × 8½"

Cut for block C:

- 7 squares 2½" × 2½" for centers

- 14 rectangles 1½" × 2½" and 14 rectangles 1½" × 4½"

- 14 rectangles 2½" × 4½" and 14 rectangles 2½" × 8½"

Cut for block D:

- 5 squares 2½" × 2½" for centers

- 10 rectangles 2½" × 3½" and 10 rectangles 3½" × 8½"

Cut for block E:

- 5 squares 4½" × 4½" for centers

- 10 rectangles 1½" × 4½" and 10 rectangles 1½" × 6½"

- 10 rectangles 1½" × 6½" and 10 rectangles 1½" × 8½"

Cut for block F:

- 11 squares 4½" × 4½" for centers

- 22 rectangles 2½" × 4½" and 22 rectangles 2½" × 8½"

Cut for block G:

- 5 squares 2½" × 2½"

- 10 rectangles 1½" × 2½" and 10 rectangles 1½" × 4½"

- 10 rectangles 1½" × 4½" and 10 rectangles 1½" × 6½"

- 10 rectangles 1½" × 6½" and 10 rectangles 1½" × 8½"

Piecing

Piece the blocks as shown. Press.

BLOCK A

Step 1

Step 2; make 11.

BLOCK B

Step 1

Step 2

Step 3

Step 4; make 12.

BLOCK C

Step 1

Step 2

Step 3

Step 4; make 7.

BLOCK D

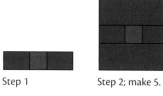

Step 1   Step 2; make 5.

BLOCK E

Step 1   Step 2

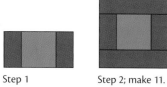

Step 3   Step 4; make 5.

BLOCK F

Step 1   Step 2; make 11.

BLOCK G

Step 1   Step 2   Step 3

Step 4   Step 5

Step 6; make 5.

Putting It All Together

Refer to Putting It All Together diagram (below).

quilt center

1. Arrange and sew together the blocks in 8 rows of 7 blocks each. Press.

2. Sew together the rows. Press.

finishing

1. Layer the quilt with batting and backing. Baste or pin. See Layering the Quilt (page 6).

2. Quilt as desired, and bind.

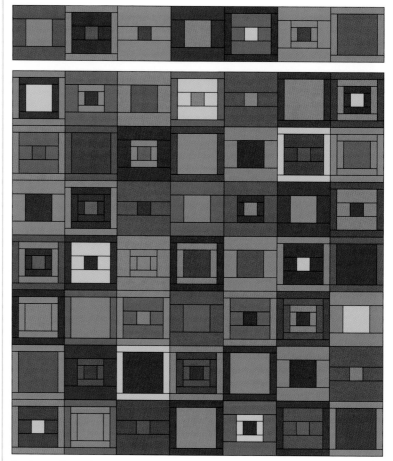

Putting It All Together

Black Button
Wall Quilt

*Big black buttons act as flower centers
in this easy-to-piece wall quilt.*

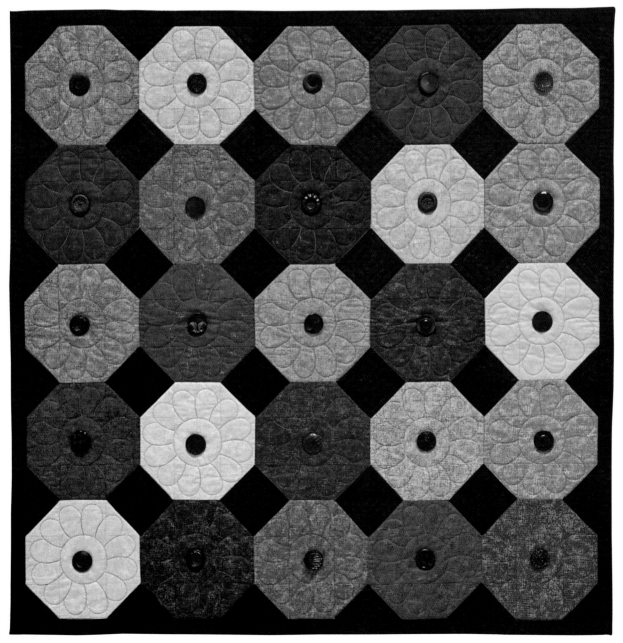

Quilted by Diane Minkley of Patched Works, Inc.

MATERIALS

¼ yard each of 25 different brights for pieced blocks

1 yard black for pieced blocks and border

3⅜ yards for backing and binding

½ yard for binding if different from backing

57" × 57" batting

25 buttons (optional)

CUTTING

Cut from each of 25 different brights for pieced blocks:

- 1 rectangle 4½" × 10½"
- 2 rectangles 3½" × 4½"
- 2 squares 3⅞" × 3⅞"; cut diagonally once to yield 4 triangles.

Cut squares diagonally.

Cut from the black:

- 50 squares 3⅞" × 3⅞"; cut diagonally once to yield 100 triangles for pieced blocks.
- 2 strips 1½" × 50½" for 2 side borders *
- 2 strips 1½" × 52½" for top and bottom borders *

* Cut 6 strips 1½" × fabric width, piece end to end (see Borders, page 6), and cut the border pieces.

Piecing

1. Sew together the black and bright triangles to form a square. Press.

Sew triangles.

2. Piece the blocks as shown. Make 25 blocks. Press.

Piece blocks.   Make 25.

Putting It All Together

Refer to Putting It All Together diagram (at right).

quilt center

Arrange and sew together the blocks in 5 rows of 5 blocks each. Sew together the rows. Press.

border

1. Sew the 2 side borders to the quilt top. Press toward the borders.

2. Sew the top and bottom borders to the quilt top. Press toward the borders.

finishing

1. Layer the quilt with batting and backing. Baste or pin. See Layering the Quilt (page 6).

2. Quilt as desired, and bind.

3. Add buttons if desired.

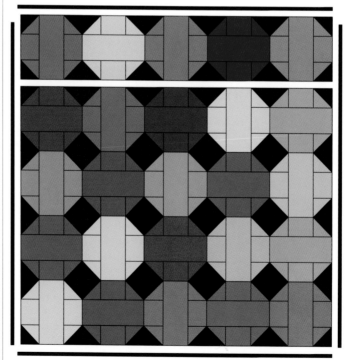

Putting It All Together

Retro Squares
Wall Quilt

Simple, framed squares are surrounded by a wide border, giving this quilt a look of timeless appeal. In each block, the center Four-Patch is framed by sets of four rectangles of contrasting colors.

Quilted by Diane Minkley of Patched Works, Inc.

◼ MATERIALS

⅜ yard each of light gray, pink, teal, light yellow, and tan for pieced blocks

⅞ yard red for pieced blocks

3 yards black for pieced blocks, lattice strips, and border

4 yards for backing and binding

½ yard for binding if different from backing

69″ × 69″ batting

◼ CUTTING

The pieces for each set of rectangles are listed together.

Cut from light gray, pink, teal, light yellow, and tan for pieced blocks:

- 32 squares 2½″ × 2½″ for centers
- 32 rectangles 1½″ × 4½″ and 32 rectangles 1½″ × 6½″
- 32 rectangles 1½″ × 8½″ and 32 rectangles 1½″ × 10½″

Cut from red for pieced blocks:

- 32 rectangles 1½″ × 6½″ and 32 rectangles 1½″ × 8½″

Cut from black (first cut border and lattice pieces on the lengthwise grain):

- 32 squares 2½″ × 2½″ for pieced block centers
- 12 rectangles 2½″ × 10½″ for lattice
- 3 strips 2½″ × 46½″ for lattice
- 2 strips 9½″ × 46½″ for 2 side borders
- 2 strips 9½″ × 64½″ for top and bottom borders

Piecing

Piece the blocks as shown. Press.

Step 1

Step 2

Step 3

Step 4

Step 5

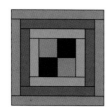

Step 6

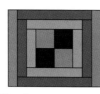

Step 7

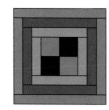

Make 10.

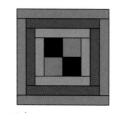

Make 6.

Putting It All Together

Refer to Putting It All Together diagram (page 33).

quilt center

1. Arrange the blocks in 4 rows of 4 blocks each.

2. Sew the vertical lattice strips between the blocks. Press.

3. Sew the horizontal lattice strips between the rows. Press.

border

1. Sew the 2 side borders to the quilt top. Press toward the borders.

2. Sew the top and bottom borders to the quilt top. Press toward the borders.

finishing

1. Layer the quilt with batting and backing. Baste or pin. See Layering the Quilt (page 6).

2. Quilt as desired, and bind.

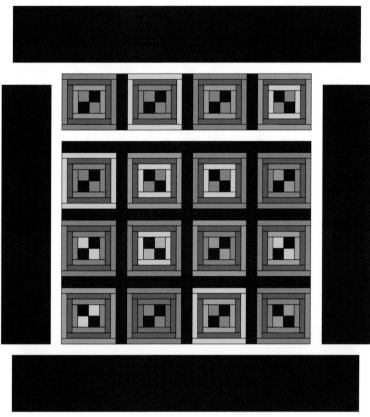

Putting It All Together

Buttons in the Rough

Wall Quilt

I am a long-time button collector and love to design projects that show off some of my favorites. The buttons on this quilt wanted out of the jar. This simple quilt was made to show them off.

Quilted by Diane Minkley of Patched Works, Inc.

MATERIALS

¾ yard total assorted brights for pieced center

¼ yard gray for inner border

⅞ yard black for pieced center and outer border

1¼ yards for backing and binding

⅜ yard for binding if different from backing

39″ × 39″ batting

36 buttons (optional)

CUTTING

Cut from assorted brights for pieced center:

- 25 squares 4½″ × 4½″

Cut from black:

- 2 squares 15″ × 15″; cut diagonally once to yield 4 triangles for pieced center.

Cut squares diagonally.

- 2 strips 2½″ × 30¾″ for 2 side outer borders

- 2 strips 2½″ × 34¾″ for top and bottom outer borders

Cut from gray:

- 2 strips 1½″ × 28¾″ for 2 side inner borders

- 2 strips 1½″ × 30¾″ for top and bottom inner borders

Putting It All Together

Refer to Putting It All Together diagram (at right).

quilt center

1. Arrange and sew together the squares in 5 rows of 5 squares each. Press.

2. Sew together the rows. Press.

3. Sew 2 triangles to the pieced center on opposite sides along the long side of the triangle. Press.

4. Sew the 2 remaining triangles to the quilt top. Press.

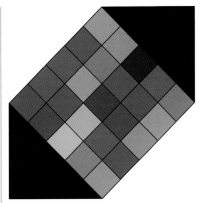

Sew triangles to pieced center.

inner border

1. Sew the 2 side borders to the quilt top. Press toward the borders.

2. Sew the top and bottom borders to the quilt top. Press toward the borders.

outer border

1. Sew the 2 side borders to the quilt top. Press toward the borders.

2. Sew the top and bottom borders to the quilt top. Press toward the borders.

finishing

1. Layer the quilt with batting and backing. Baste or pin. See Layering the Quilt (page 6).

2. Quilt as desired, and bind.

3. Add buttons if desired.

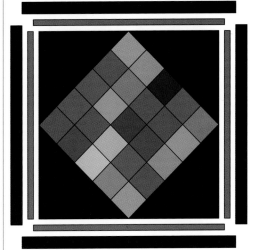

Putting It All Together

Big Blooms
Table Topper

Brighten up your table with the Big Blooms table topper. A colorful pieced border surrounds five big blooms for a topper with folk art charm. The pieced background adds even more texture.

Quilted by Diane Minkley of Patched Works, Inc.

MATERIALS

1⅛ yards tan for pieced appliqué background

1⅛ yards light for pieced appliqué background

½ yard each of 5 brights for flower petals and pieced border

¾ yard total assorted brights for flower centers and pieced border

⅜ yard black for flower pistils and pieced border corners

3½ yards paper-backed fusible web

3⅛ yards for backing and binding

½ yard for binding if different from backing

53″ × 53″ batting

CUTTING

Cut from tan for pieced background:

- 16 squares 5½″ × 5½″
- 16 squares 5⅞″ × 5⅞″; cut diagonally once to yield 32 triangles.

Cut squares diagonally.

Cut from the light for pieced background:

- 16 squares 5½″ × 5½″
- 16 squares 5⅞″ × 5⅞″; cut diagonally once to yield 32 triangles.

Cut from the assorted brights: 64 rectangles 3″ × 4½″ for pieced border

Cut from the black: 4 squares 4½″ × 4½″ for border corners

Piecing

Sew together the tan and light triangles to form a square. Make 16 squares. Press.

Sew triangles. Make 16.

Putting It All Together

Refer to Putting It All Together diagram (page 38).

quilt center

1. Arrange and sew together the squares and pieced squares into 8 rows of 8 squares each. Press.

2. Sew together the rows. Press.

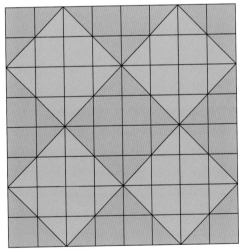

Piece table topper background.

Appliqué

1. Trace the partial pattern on pattern pullout pages P57–P60; reverse the pattern and trace to make a full pattern and cut:

    5 each of pattern pieces 1 and 2

    40 of pattern piece 3

2. Appliqué the appropriate pieces to the background.

pieced border

1. Arrange and sew together 4 rows of 16 rectangles each for the pieced borders. Press.

2. Sew the 2 side borders to the table topper. Press toward the borders.

3. Sew a corner square on each end of the remaining borders. Press.

4. Sew the top and bottom borders to the table topper. Press toward the borders.

finishing

1. Layer the table topper with batting and backing. Baste or pin. See Layering the Quilt (page 6).

2. Quilt as desired, and bind.

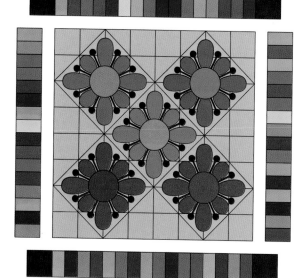

Putting It All Together

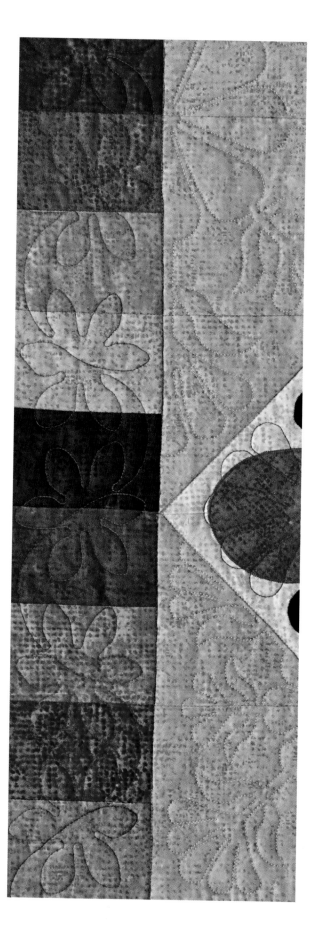

Boardwalk
— Table Runner —

*Bright, pieced blocks are surrounded by appliqué and a pieced
jewel-toned border to give this runner a rich, lush look.*

Quilted by Diane Minkley of Patched Works, Inc.

▓ MATERIALS

⅛ yard each of 13 assorted brights for pieced blocks

¾ yard black for pieced blocks

¼ yard red for pieced blocks

⅓ yard tan for appliqué

¾ yard total assorted darks for pieced border

½ yard paper-backed fusible web

1¾ yards for backing and binding

⅜ yard for binding if different from backing

60″ × 30″ batting

▓ CUTTING

Cut from assorted brights: 13 strips 1½″ × width of fabric for pieced blocks

Cut from black: 12 squares 7″ × 7″ for pieced blocks

Cut from assorted darks: 28 squares 5½″ × 5½″ for pieced border

Cut from red:

- 6 strips 1½″ × 13½″ for pieced blocks
- 6 strips 1½″ × 15½″ for pieced blocks

Piecing

1. Arrange and sew together 13 strips of assorted brights. Carefully press. The sewn strips should measure 13½″ × the width of the fabric.

Sew strips together.

2. Cut the sewn strips into 3 squares 13½″ × 13½″.

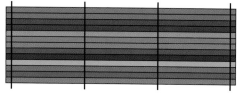

Cut 3 squares 13½″ × 13½″.

3. Using a light-colored fabric pencil, draw a diagonal line on the wrong side of each of the black 7″ squares.

4. With right sides together, layer a black 7″ square over 2 opposite corners of the pieced 13½″ × 13½″ square. Stitch the layered squares together on the drawn lines. Trim to ¼″ from the stitched lines. Press.

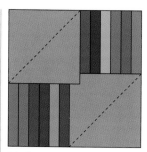

Stitch on drawn line.

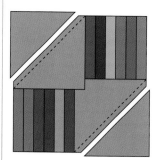

Trim.

5. Repeat Step 4, placing a black 7″ square over the remaining 2 corners of each pieced 13½″ × 13½″ square. Trim and press.

6. Sew a 1½″ × 13½″ strip to opposite sides of the pieced block. Press.

7. Sew the 2 strips 1½″ × 15½″ to the remaining sides of the pieced block. Press.

Piece blocks. Make 2.

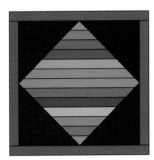

Piece block. Make 1.

Appliqué

1. Use the patterns on pattern pullout pages P61–P64 to cut:

12 of pattern piece 1

24 of pattern piece 2

2. Appliqué the appropriate pieces to the blocks.

Appliqué blocks.

Putting It All Together

Refer to Putting It All Together diagram (below).

quilt center

Arrange and sew together the blocks in 1 row of 3 blocks. Press.

pieced border

1. Arrange and sew together 2 rows of 9 squares each for the 2 side borders. Press.

2. Sew the 2 side borders to the runner top. Press.

3. Arrange and sew together 2 rows of 5 squares each for the 2 end borders. Press.

4. Sew the 2 end borders to the runner top. Press.

finishing

1. Layer the table runner with batting and backing. Baste or pin. See Layering the Quilt (page 6).

2. Quilt as desired, and bind.

Putting It All Together

Checkered Whimsy
Table Runner

The color combination of purples, greens, and teals gives this table runner a light-hearted, whimsical look.

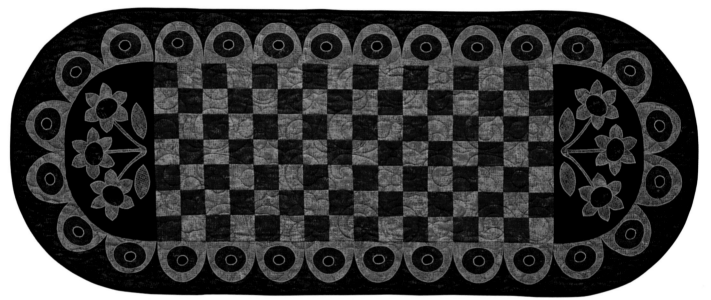

Quilted by Diane Minkley of Patched Works, Inc.

MATERIALS

⅜ yard light green for pieced center

⅜ yard light purple for pieced center

¼ yard black for appliqué background and appliquéd circles

1 yard dark green for appliqué backgrounds

⅛ yard green for stems and leaves

⅛ yard teal for flowers

⅛ yard dark teal for flower centers

½ yard light teal for scallops

¼ yard dark purple for circles

2 yards paper-backed fusible web

1¾ yards for backing

½ yard for bias binding

27″ × 59″ batting

CUTTING

Cut from light green: 56 squares 2½″ × 2½″ for pieced center

Cut from light purple: 56 squares 2½″ × 2½″ for pieced center

Cut from dark green: 2 strips 4½″ × 32½″ for appliqué backgrounds

Piecing

1. Arrange and sew together 4 light purple and 3 light green squares for the pieced center. Press. Make 8 rows.

Sew squares. Make 8.

2. Arrange and sew together 4 light green and 3 light purple squares for the pieced center. Press. Make 8 rows.

Sew squares. Make 8.

Appliqué

1. Trace the partial pattern on pattern pullout pages P57–P60; reverse and trace to make a full pattern and cut:

2 of pattern piece 1

2 of pattern piece 2

2 and 2 reverse of pattern piece 3

2 of pattern piece 4

6 each of pattern pieces 5 and 6

2 and 2 reverse each of pattern pieces 7, 8, and 9

16 of pattern piece 10

28 each of pattern pieces 11 and 12

2. Appliqué the appropriate pieces to the backgrounds.

Appliqué table runner ends. Make 2.

Appliqué table runner sides. Make 2.

Putting It All Together

Refer to Putting It All Together diagram (at right).

quilt center

Arrange and sew together 16 rows of squares to form the pieced center of the table runner. Press.

border

1. Sew the 2 runner sides to the pieced center. Press toward the borders.

2. Sew the 2 runner ends to the pieced center. Press toward the runner ends.

finishing

1. Layer the table runner with batting and backing. Baste or pin. See Layering the Quilt (page 6).

2. Quilt as desired, and bind.

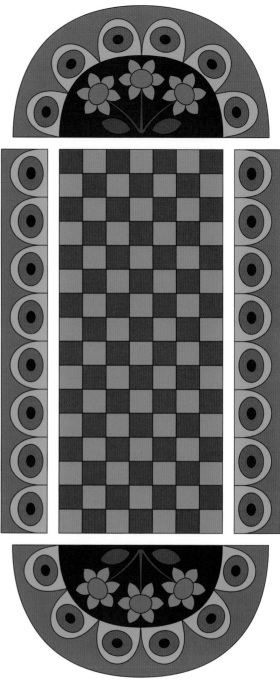

Putting It All Together

Half Moon Rising
Table Runner

*Appliquéd circles in tan, black, and grays make up the center of this table runner.
The red pieced border gives the runner a classic look with timeless appeal.*

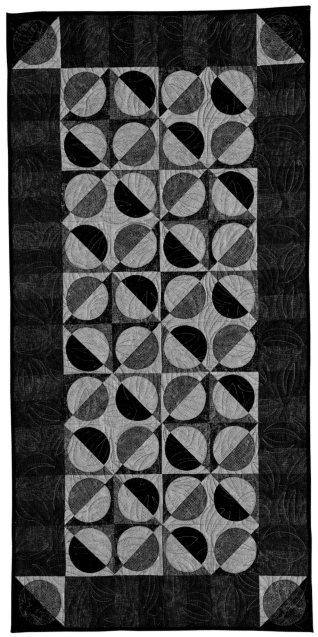

Quilted by Diane Minkley of Patched Works, Inc.

◐ MATERIALS

1 yard light tan for appliqué backgrounds and appliquéd half circles

½ yard light gray for appliqué backgrounds and appliquéd half circles

⅜ yard dark gray for appliqué backgrounds and appliquéd half circles

⅜ yard black for appliqué backgrounds and appliquéd half circles

⅜ yard dark red for pieced border

⅜ yard red for pieced border

1¾ yards paper-backed fusible web

1⅝ yards for backing and binding

⅜ yard for binding if different from backing

29″ × 53″ batting

◐ CUTTING

Cut for appliqué block backgrounds:

Cut from light tan: 22 squares 4⅞″ × 4⅞″; cut diagonally once to yield 44 triangles.

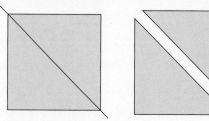

Cut squares diagonally.

Cut from light gray: 10 squares 4⅞″ × 4⅞″; cut diagonally once to yield 20 triangles.

Cut from dark gray: 10 squares 4⅞″ × 4⅞″; cut diagonally once to yield 20 triangles.

Cut from black: 2 squares 4⅞″ × 4⅞″; cut diagonally once to yield 4 triangles.

Cut from red: 28 rectangles 2½″ × 4½″ for pieced border

Cut from dark red: 28 rectangles 2½″ × 4½″ for pieced border

Appliqué

1. Use the patterns on pattern pullout pages P61–P64 to cut 88 of pattern piece 1. Note: The pattern includes the seam allowance for the diagonal edge of the triangle background.

2. Cut 40 light tan, 24 light gray, 4 dark gray, and 20 black.

3. Appliqué the half circles on the triangle backgrounds.

Make 20.

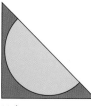

Make 20.

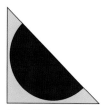

Make 20.

Make 4.

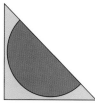

Make 24.

Piecing

Arrange and sew together the triangles to make the blocks. Press.

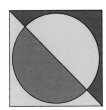

Make 20.

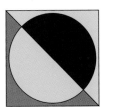

Make 20.

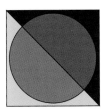

Make 4.

Putting It All Together

Refer to Putting It All Together diagram (at right).

quilt center

1. Arrange and sew together the blocks in 10 rows of 4 blocks each. Press.

2. Sew together the rows to form the center of the table runner. Press.

pieced border

1. Arrange and sew together 2 rows of 20 rectangles 2½″ × 4½″ each for the 2 side borders. Press.

2. Sew the 2 side borders to the table runner. Press toward the borders.

3. Arrange and sew together 2 rows of 8 rectangles 2½″ × 4½″ each for the end borders. Press.

4. Sew an appliqué block on each end of the 2 end borders. Press.

5. Sew the end borders to the table runner. Press toward the borders.

finishing

1. Layer the table runner with batting and backing. Baste or pin. See Layering the Quilt (page 6).

2. Quilt as desired, and bind

Putting It All Together

Gold Coast
Mini-Quilt

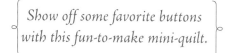

Show off some favorite buttons
with this fun-to-make mini-quilt.

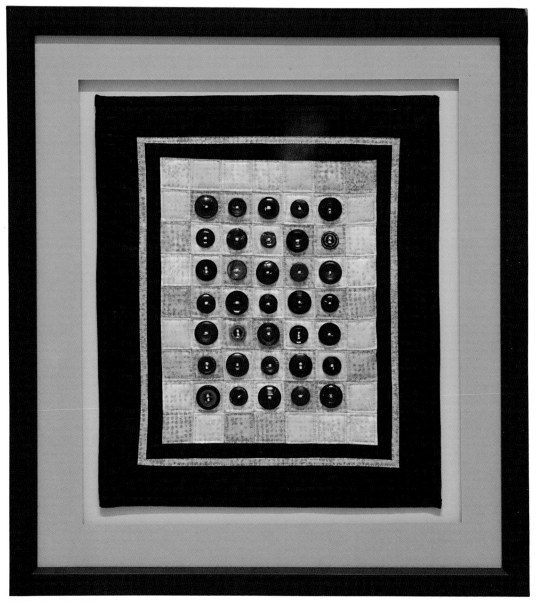

Quilted by Kim Schaefer.

MATERIALS

¼ yard total assorted lights for piecing and middle border

⅝ yard black for inner and outer borders, backing, and binding

15″ × 17″ batting

35 buttons (optional)

CUTTING

Cut from assorted lights:

- 63 squares 1½″ × 1½″
- 2 strips ¾″ × 10½″ for 2 side middle borders
- 2 strips ¾″ × 9″ for top and bottom middle borders

Cut from black:

- 2 strips 1″ × 9½″ for 2 side inner borders
- 2 strips 1″ × 8½″ for top and bottom inner borders
- 2 strips 1½″ × 11″ for 2 side outer borders
- 2 strips 1½″ × 11″ for top and bottom outer borders

Putting It All Together

Refer to Putting It All Together diagram (at right).

quilt center

Arrange and sew together the squares in 9 rows of 7 squares each. Sew together the rows. Press.

borders

Inner border

1. Sew the 2 side borders to the mini-quilt. Press toward the borders.

2. Sew the top and bottom borders to the mini-quilt. Press toward the borders.

Middle border

1. Sew the 2 side borders to the mini-quilt. Press toward the borders.

2. Sew the top and bottom borders to the mini-quilt. Press toward the borders.

Outer border

1. Sew the 2 side borders to the mini-quilt. Press toward the borders.

2. Sew the top and bottom borders to the mini-quilt. Press toward the borders.

finishing

1. Layer the mini-quilt with batting and backing. Baste or pin. See Layering the Quilt (page 6).

2. Quilt as desired, and bind.

3. Add buttons if desired.

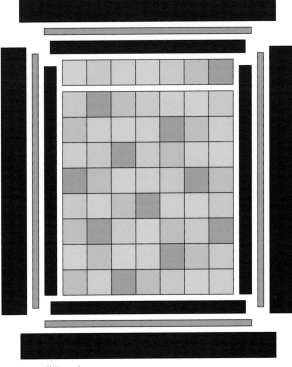

Putting It All Together

Button Flower
Mini-Quilt

Embellish a mini-quilt with buttons for a fast and fun project to decorate your home.

Quilted by Kim Schaefer.

MATERIALS

⅓ yard black for appliqué background and backing

Scraps for appliqué pieces

¼ yard paper-backed fusible web

⅛ yard for binding

14″ × 14″ batting

60 buttons approximately (optional)

CUTTING

Cut from black: 1 square 10½″ × 10½″ for appliqué background

Appliqué

1. Use the patterns on pattern pullout pages P61–P64 to cut:

- 1 each of pattern pieces 1 through 17
- 15 of pattern piece 18

2. Appliqué the appropriate pieces onto the background.

Putting It All Together

Refer to Putting It All Together diagram (at right).

finishing

1. Layer the mini-quilt with batting and backing. Baste or pin. See Layering the Quilt (page 6).

2. Quilt as desired, and bind.

3. Add buttons if desired.

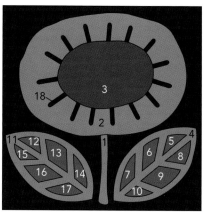

Putting It All Together

All Framed Up
Mini-Quilt

*With or without buttons, this mini-quilt done
in neutral fabrics will enhance any decor.*

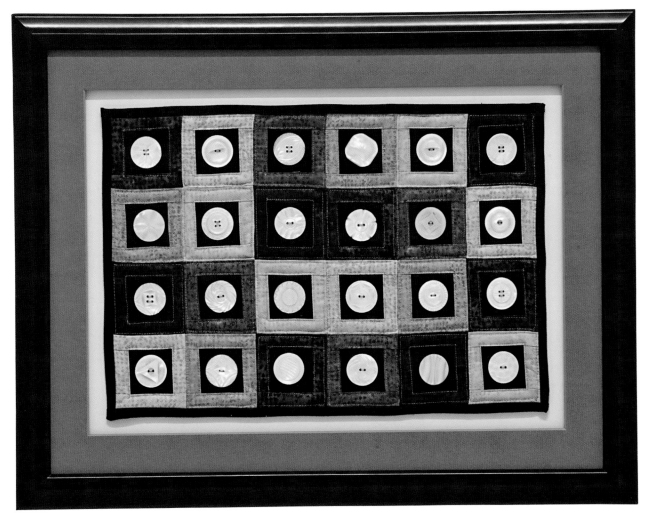

Quilted by Kim Schaefer.

◉ MATERIALS

¼ yard black for pieced blocks

⅓ yard total assorted creams, tans, browns, and grays for pieced blocks

⅝ yard for backing and binding

19″ × 14″ batting

24 buttons (optional)

◉ CUTTING

Cut from black: 24 squares 2″ × 2″ for pieced blocks

Cut from assorted creams, tans, browns, and grays for pieced blocks matching pairs of each size:

- 48 rectangles 1″ × 2″
- 48 rectangles 1″ × 3″

Piecing

Piece the blocks as shown. Make 24 blocks.

Piece blocks.

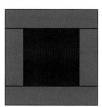

Make 24.

Putting It All Together

Refer to Putting It All Together diagram (below).

quilt center

1. Arrange and sew together the blocks in 4 rows of 6 blocks each. Press.

2. Sew together the rows. Press.

finishing

1. Layer the mini-quilt with batting and backing. Baste or pin. See Layering the Quilt (page 6).

2. Quilt as desired, and bind.

3. Add buttons if desired.

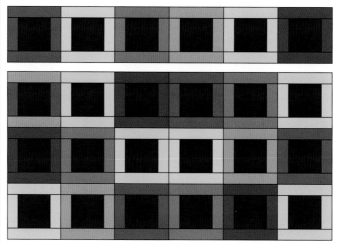

Putting It All Together

Button Bars
Mini-Quilt

A colorful, pieced border frames this mini-quilt. The bars are raw-edge appliquéd to make this a fast and fun project.

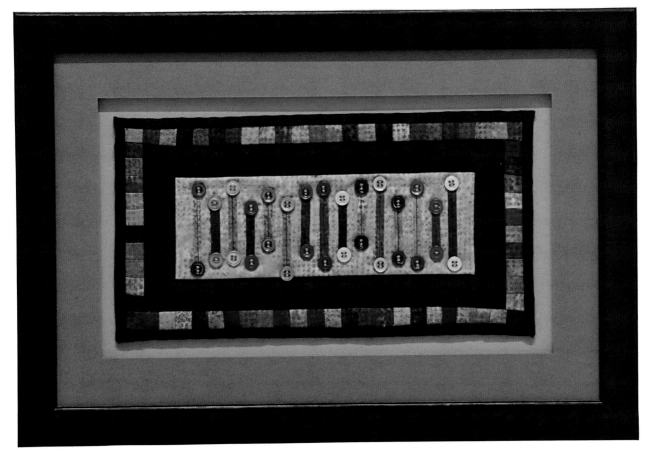

Quilted by Kim Schaefer.

MATERIALS

⅛ yard tan for appliqué background

⅛ yard black for inner border

⅛ yard total assorted brights for appliqué and pieced border

⅛ yard paper-backed fusible web

⅜ yard backing and binding

16″ × 10″ batting

30 buttons (optional)

CUTTING

Cut from tan: 1 rectangle 3½″ × 9½″ for background

Cut from black:

- 2 rectangles 1½″ × 3½″ for 2 side borders
- 2 rectangles 1½″ × 11½″ for top and bottom borders

Cut from assorted brights: 68 squares 1″ × 1″ for pieced border

Piecing

inner border

1. Sew the 2 side borders to the background. Press toward the borders.

2. Sew the top and bottom borders to the background. Press toward the borders.

outer pieced border

1. Arrange and sew together 2 rows of 10 squares each for the 2 side borders. Press.

2. Sew the 2 side borders to the mini-quilt. Press toward the borders.

3. Arrange and sew together 2 rows of 24 squares each for the top and bottom borders. Press.

4. Sew the top and bottom borders to the mini-quilt. Press toward the borders.

Appliqué

1. Use the patterns on pattern pullout pages P61–P64 to cut:

  1 each of pattern pieces 1 and 2

  5 of pattern piece 3

  2 of pattern piece 4

  3 each of pattern pieces 5 and 6

2. Appliqué the appropriate pieces onto the background. For raw-edge appliqué, sew a line down the center of the appliqué pieces.

Putting It All Together

Refer to Putting It All Together diagram (below).

finishing

1. Layer the mini-quilt with batting and backing. Baste or pin. See Layering the Quilt (page 6).

2. Quilt as desired, and bind.

3. Add buttons if desired.

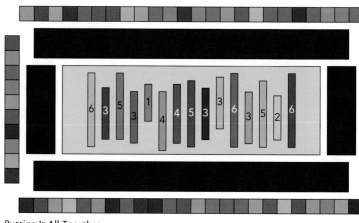

Putting It All Together

About the Author

Kim Schaefer is from southeastern Wisconsin, where she lives with her husband, Gary, her son, Gator, and her dog, Rio. Kim and Gary also have two daughters, Cody and Ali, and three college-bound sons, Max, Ben, and Sam. Kim has two stepdaughters, Danielle and Tina, and two stepsons, Gary Jr. and Dax.

Kim began sewing at an early age, which Kim says was a nightmare for her mom, who continually and patiently untangled bobbin messes. Kim was formally educated at the University of Wisconsin in Milwaukee, where she studied fine arts and majored in fiber. At age 23, Kim took her first quilting class and was immediately hooked.

In 1996, Little Quilt Company made its debut at Quilt Market in Minneapolis. In addition to designing quilt patterns, Kim designs fabric for Andover/Makower and works with Leo Licensing, which licenses her designs for nonfabric products.

Previous books by Kim Schaefer:

Above book is also available as an eBook.

Above book is also available as an eBook.

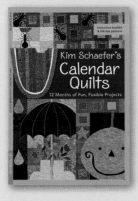

Great Titles *from* C&T PUBLISHING

Available at your local retailer or **www.ctpub.com** *or* **800-284-1114**

For a list of other fine books from C&T Publishing, visit our website to view our catalog online.

C&T PUBLISHING, INC.
P.O. Box 1456
Lafayette, CA 94549
800-284-1114

Email: ctinfo@ctpub.com
Website: www.ctpub.com

C&T Publishing's professional photography services are now available to the public. Visit us at www.ctmediaservices.com.

Tips and Techniques can be found at www.ctpub.com > Consumer Resources > Quiltmaking Basics: Tips & Techniques for Quiltmaking & More

For quilting supplies:

COTTON PATCH
1025 Brown Ave.
Lafayette, CA 94549
Store: 925-284-1177
Mail order: 925-283-7883

Email: CottonPa@aol.com
Website: www.quiltusa.com

Note: Fabrics used in the quilts shown may not be currently available, as fabric manufacturers keep most fabrics in print for only a short time.